Marco

How to be a stoic

*Overcome anxiety, criticism and remain
humble against difficulties*

"It is time for you to realize that you have something more powerful and miraculous within you than the things that affect you and make you dance like a puppet."

Marcus Aurelius

Table of contents

Introduction

What is Stoicism?

In 301 BC, a Phoenician merchant named Zeno came to Athens from the city of Cilium, Cyprus, and founded a school of ancient philosophy there, called the School of Athens. This school was very important because it was the first to deal with Stoicism. There were many competing schools of thought based on the life and thought of Socrates, who was the most famous Athenian philosopher of the time, and Stoicism was one of them.

Zionism was the original name of this philosophy, but it was changed to "Stoicism" because Zeno and his followers used to meet in the Stoa Pokily, or "Painted Porch", a colonnade decorated with mythical and historical battle scenes. It was on the north side of the agora, the ancient Athenian market place, that Zeno lived.

Like their hero, Socrates, the Stoics met in the public square, under this famous porch, where everyone could hear them debate. This was different from the other formal schools of Athenian philosophy, which met in the library. It is said that Zeno walked around the porch while he was speaking, so that it was not occupied by slouching people. The term "Stoic philosophy" has been taken to mean a "philosophy of the street", a philosophy for people who are not locked in the "ivory towers" of academia. Indeed, until recently, the Stoics have not received much attention from modern philosophy departments.

Before the 20th century, people learning philosophy were likely to read works by Stoic philosophers. But philosophy did not just lose interest in Stoicism in the 20th century. It even lost interest in philosophies of life in general. It was possible, as my own experience shows, to take philosophy courses for a decade without reading the Stoics or thinking about philosophies of life, let alone adopting one.

Because of the success of cognitive behavioral therapy, Stoicism has become more popular since the 1970s.

However, in the ancient world, as we have seen, Stoicism was one of the most important and respected schools of thought for nearly five centuries. It is said that the Athenians loved Zeno so much that they gave him the keys to their city and built him a bronze statue.

The death of Socrates was very different from that of Zenon. It is assumed that the Athenians approved a golden crown and a tomb built at public expense to honor his virtue and self-discipline. This public

statement praised his many years of study of phi
in Athens and stated that he was a good person
respect. He taught virtue and self-discipline to th
people who came to him for instruction, directed them
to what was best, and gave everyone, by his own
conduct, a model to imitate in perfect harmony with his
teaching.

This is why the Stoics were interested in the way
Zeno behaved. They thought that emulation of the wise
and the good was the best way to learn philosophy, so
they tried to follow them. Zeno initially led a simple and
austere life like the Cynical philosophers. This had a
great impact on Stoicism. As a result, Zeno's reputation
for self-control (supplication) would become famous,
even legendary. People could be praised for their own
self-discipline by comparing it to Zeno's. Among other
things, an anonymous ancient poet wrote about him:

The cold of winter and the incessant rain, he will
not be able to defend himself. The fierce rays of the
summer sun will not be able to bend this iron frame. It
does not take part in the public feast and jubilation: It
waits patiently all night and all day. Do not abandon his
study of philosophy. (Life, 7.27)

If you want to be a good person, you must study
ethics, physics and logic. This is where Zeno goes
against his original allegiance to cynicism. As we shall
see, the Cynics also thought that all external things were
ultimately "indifferent". The Stoics, on the other hand,
took a more subtle approach, allowing them to

3

appreciate some conventional things while maintaining a sense of separation from them.

Although they were very interested in the application of philosophy to real-life problems, the Stoics were also very interested in the Socratic question: How can one live a good life? They saw themselves as true warriors of the mind, and perhaps they thought that modern academic philosophy was nothing but sophistry, that is, a set of arguments and reasonings that were false despite an appearance of truth.

Part 1

How I discovered this new trend

Chapter 1

The history of Stoicism in brief

During the Hellenistic period in the Mediterranean, Stoicism was one of the most important schools of thought in the region. The word "Hellenic" means "one who speaks Greek". This period is marked by the death of Alexander the Great in 323 B.C. Some believe it ended in 146 B.C., when Rome invaded the heart of Greece, while most people agree that it ended in 31 B.C.

"Hellenistic" is a word we use to describe a period of history. We can also speak of "Hellenistic schools of thought" or "Hellenistic philosophies". At that time, the Athenians, where Stoicism was born, were making many new things, and proposing new ideas. History has never seen anything like it, and we have it to thank for much of what we appreciate today.

It is important to know that this time in Ancient Greece saw great changes in art, theater, mathematics, science, music, literature and, of course, philosophy. The Cynics, Skeptics and Epicureans are just a few of the schools of thought that existed at that time, as well as Stoicism, which was a philosophy known to many people.

This brings us to the beginnings of Stoicism.

Zeno of Cilium is considered the founder of the Stoic school of thought. The wealthy merchant Zeno was on his way to Athens when he was shipwrecked. He had with him purple dye, in large quantities. In the past, people thought that this color was a sign of wealth and luxury, because this dye had to be carefully extracted from sea snails. Zeno's money therefore theoretically came from the sea and this money somehow returned to the sea because of the shipwreck.

So, Zeno was now stuck in Athens. Legend has it that Zeno went to meet the Oracle of Delphi to get help from the God Apollo. This is what any of us would have done at that time as well. There, the Oracle told him that he should "dye himself with the color, not of dead shells, but of dead men", and that he should dwell on it.

Zeno thought this meant that he should learn from the great thinkers of the past, and so he began to read about people like Socrates. This is important because Stoic philosophy is thought to be based on the teachings of Socrates, which emphasize virtue as the main benefit of life.

Zeno then studied with Cratus for a few years before founding his own school of philosophy in 300 BC on the steps of the famous painted porch in Athens called the Stoa Pokily discussed earlier. This is where

Stoicism was born: a philosophy that asserts that a good life is one that is based on virtue and is lived in harmony with nature.

It was not until Stoicism made its way to Rome that a great deal of literature began to emerge on the subject. During this period, many important philosophers led the Stoic school and added to the ideas that Zeno already had. Three people were the representatives of the Stoic school: Zeno, Cleanthe and Chrysopsis. We can also mention Diogenes of Babylon, who went to Rome in 155 BC with Stoicism and other philosophers in mind, which he spread throughout the Roman Empire.

So, in Roman times we have excellent writings from four great Stoic thinkers who came from very different places in Rome.

To begin with, we have Seneca the Younger, who was a Roman politician, as well as an investor, advisor and playwright. When we look at Seneca's writings, we can see two different types of people: one who was very interested in philosophy and one who was trying to figure out what was right and wrong. Seneca was unfortunately caught up in many scandals during his life, because he was very close to Nero, one of the most oppressive emperors in Rome.

Even though he had his faults, one cannot say that Seneca was not thoughtful. I think he is the best Stoic we can draw on even today. He was a person who struggled to live by his own teachings, which made him very human. People of all times love to read his most popular writings, because they are full of good thoughts.

One of his most popular works are the letters he wrote to a friend, Lucilius, on how to lead a good life.

Musonius Rufus is the next of the main Roman philosophers we can read about today on Stoicism. Most of what we know about Musonius comes from a few short stories he wrote. These stories can help us learn more about a man who was interested not only in the profound ideas of Stoicism, but also in the very practical day-to-day application of this philosophy. Sometimes even too practical. For example, a Stoic might argue for hours about whether a man should cut off his beard because it showed that he was a man.

Then we come to Epictetus, a student of Musonius Rufus, who was also a teacher. Epictetus was a slave when he was young, and his name means "earned" or "acquired". Later, he was freed by his master, who saw in him many intellectual abilities. It was then that he went to Musonius Rufus and learned from him. Epictetus is considered one of the most important Stoic masters, and what we have of him is a collection of speeches recorded by a man called Arrien of Nicomedia. He also put together the "best of Epictetus", which he called the Enchiridion.

We will now turn our attention to Marcus Aurelius, who is one of the best-known Stoics. He was also a great fan of Epictetus.

Marcus Aurelius is the last of the "five good Roman emperors". It all started when he was very young. He and his brother, Lucius Verus, were both trained to become emperors of Rome. It didn't matter that Marcus' brother had no real interest in running a government. His love of philosophy and his knowledge of the teachings of Epictetus led him to do his job as emperor in the best possible way.

It is partly because of this that we can see the power of philosophy and stoicism.

During his time as emperor, he could have had anything he wanted. He could have snapped his fingers and killed anyone he didn't like. But he was first a philosopher, then an emperor. A journal entitled "Meditations" that he kept shows us that he lived by the right rules. When we look at this collection of Marcus Aurelius' thoughts, we can see that he was not happy to be the ruler of the country. He was always manipulated and deceived by other people. It was very difficult for him to keep the power he had from going to his head, but still, he managed to control himself.

A philosophy of all times

I want to emphasize the fact that all the Stoics I have mentioned had very different lives. Zeno lost everything in his shipwreck. Seneca was very rich and powerful. Epictetus was a slave. Marcus Aurelius was an emperor. This is a true testament to the fact that Stoicism is a philosophy that was born in adversity and shaped by the ups and downs of life.

If you want to be a good person at any time in your life, you should follow this philosophy. If you follow stoicism, you can learn to intelligently handle the best and worst events that happen in your life. Stoicism is said to have influenced some very famous people such as Thomas Jefferson, Theodore Roosevelt, James Stockdale, John Steinbeck, JK Rowling, and even Nelson Mandela, who is said to have been inspired by the Stoics while he was in prison.

Even though we are in the 21st century, we are still trying to understand how useful and effective Stoicism can be in our lives. So it's up to you and me to step in. It's our job to see if these ancient ideas are true or not, applicable or not. To do what the ancient Stoics did, we need to add philosophy to our lives and get the best ideas from it.

To extend this great and long-standing philosophy to as many people as possible, I hope you will join me. Let us try it, improve it and share it together.

Origin and representative of the Stoa

The Stoa originated in Athens during the Hellenistic period, around 300 BC, and was founded by Zeno. Its name comes from a brightly painted pillared hall (Greek: ion. πion., stoa pokily = colored pillared hall) in the market place of Athens, in which Zeno started his teaching activities.

In the Stoa, ethical questions were dealt with, such as:

- "What is good for society?"
- "How does one become happy as an individual?"

Important Greek representatives of the Stoa were:

- Cleanthe (ca. 300 BC)
- Chrysopoeia (around 280-208 BC)
- Paneities (ca. 180-110 BC)

Important Latin representatives of the Stoa were:

- The writer and philosopher Seneca (4 BC - 65 AD)
- The philosopher and emperor Marcus Aurelius (121-180 AD)

What was the Stoics' idea of the world?

The Stoics of the time believed that all processes in the cosmos were guided by an active force, the Logos. This Logos is, in a way, comparable to God. Thanks to the Logos, everything in the world is rationally ordered; the Logos is omnipresent. All men, even slaves or barbarians, have a part of reason. They therefore carry within them a part of the Logos.

All processes in the world are predetermined by the Logos. The Stoics call this providence (Latin: providential). As a rational being, man is able to recognize and submit to his predetermined destiny. He must therefore live according to his nature (Latin: secundum natura vivere). In particular, man is by nature a being created for the community, which obliges him to lead an active life (Latin: vita active) in the service of society.

The Stoic rules of life

The Stoics derive their rules for a fulfilling life from adherence to the life predetermined by the Logos. In this diagram you will find the most important terms and rules of Stoic philosophy:

- Apathy is the absence of passion and effect, such as anger, sadness, greed, anger, external.   It means resisting your impulses and passions.
- Ataraxia is the stillness of the soul or the calmness of the soul, which cannot be influenced by effects. Therefore, you must remain calm, and not let yourself be upset by anything.
- Self-sufficiency, i.e. the state in which one is independent of other people and external goods. One must not depend on anything or anyone.

- Eudaimonia (from the Greek: luck, happiness) can only be achieved by following the above rules.

The following quote is attributed to the Stoic philosopher Epictetus, it represents well the ideology of Stoicism:

"It is not important what happens to you in life, but how you react to it".

Since life is predetermined by the Logos, man must react rationally and carefully to what happens to him. He must not let emotions such as anger, sadness or irritation tempt him to act rashly and thus endanger his peace of mind.

Chapter 2

The two pillars of Stoicism

Before examining the fundamental principles of Stoicism, let us keep in mind that it is an eminently practical and operational philosophy. Marcus Aurelius was a Stoic philosopher but also one of the greatest Roman emperors. He was not an armchair philosopher spending his time debating abstract principles. On the contrary, he was a man of action, an enlightened despot, an exceptional leader who did everything to serve and protect his fellow citizens in the most reasonable and just way possible. His philosophy helped him to remain calm while accomplishing the overwhelming task of ruling the world's largest empire, which was under attack from all sides and plagued by severe epidemics and natural disasters.

Principle #1: Stoicism and Eudemonism

The basic principle of stoicism says that men must live according to Nature, and therefore, according to their nature. Knowing that Man's nature is to be rational

17

and social, each human must therefore perfect his rational nature through the development of the cardinal virtues and treat the rest of humanity as well as possible.

Fundamentally, the Stoics believe that the necessary and sufficient condition for attaining eudaemonia ("genuine" happiness and the realization of one's full potential) is a virtuous life, placed under the sign of "arete".

The word virtue, or arete, is used here in its ancient sense. It means to excel humanly, to be a good person who follows the cardinal virtues (fundamental positive characteristics): wisdom, justice, courage, temperance.

The Stoics disagree with Aristotle, who certainly insists on the necessity of virtue, but argues that some additional external aspects, such as beauty, money or health, are also essential to eudemonia.

The Stoics treat all external aspects as indifferent, because intrinsically they do not affect moral value. Indeed, it is quite possible to be poor, to have poor health, but to be morally good, and thus to live a happy life in the Stoic sense. On the other hand, according to Aristotle, an ugly man will necessarily remain unhappy, whatever he does, because he lacks a necessary component for happiness: beauty.

Let us make an important precision. Rationally, Stoics recognize that some external aspects are desirable and help to live a good life: for example, good health, a comfortable home, a good education are elements that can help you reach a good life more easily.

So, these are privileged indifferences, in the sense that Stoics act to acquire and develop them. First, they absolutely seek perfect virtue, and second, they do what they think is right regarding their health, finances and social life.

This is how one easily distinguishes the Stoics from the Cynics. The Cynics were even more "strict" than the Stoics. Indeed, they shared the same demand for virtue, but they also thought that it was the only value in life and that, consequently, nothing else had any value. Thus, they often lived as (virtuous) wanderers. This is very commendable, but I am not sure that many people today would be attracted to this lifestyle.

Principle #2: Stoicism and the sphere of control

The other fundamental principle of Stoicism is the clear delineation between what we can control and what we cannot.

It is with this principle that Epictetus begins his manual:

"Of the things that exist, some depend on us, others do not. On us depend thoughts, impulses, desires, aversions, in short, everything in which we act; on us do

not depend bodies, money, reputation, public offices, everything in which we do not act. »

Epictetus means that the only things we control are our thoughts, our attitudes, our emotions, our impulses to act. That is, only the things that happen in our brain. These are the inner things.

But we do not control the rest of the facts, which are external things. We don't control when we were born. We do not control what other people think of us. We do not control our level of social success.

Of course, our actions have an impact on certain external events, but this impact is always limited. If a man lives a healthy lifestyle, he increases his likelihood of staying healthy but is not immune to a flu epidemic. If a politician has integrity and cares about the best interests of her fellow citizens, she tends to have excellent popularity, but this may well be reduced by the manipulations of a rival and the media, combined with poor judgment on the part of voters.

Finally, there are things where our impact is almost nil: the world economic situation, the rotation of the earth around the sun, the weather. For these circumstances, no matter what we think, no matter what we do, they happen anyway. All external events are therefore subject to an almost infinite number of external parameters, which makes them uncontrollable by our will alone.

As we have seen above, Stoics believe that external things are indifferent. Thus, a Stoic statesman regards his popularity as desired indifference and his unpopularity as unwanted indifference.

The consequence is especially important: Stoics radically accept external facts as they are and as they happen.

We began by tracing the history of Stoicism: from its birth and first developments in Greece and then in Rome, to its current revival. Then we explained the two principles of Stoicism:

- The purpose of life is to excel as a virtuous and social human being. Values such as wealth, beauty or social success are desired indifferences: desirable but not essential.
- There are things we can control and things we cannot control. We can control our thoughts, our attitudes, our emotions, our impulses to action. For the rest, our level of control is limited or non-existent.

If you feel like it, I suggest you take two minutes to think about these two basic principles. In general, how do you see things in your daily life and especially how do you deal with obstacles?

It is important to act with virtue in the main ideas of Stoicism. This means that one who loves glory, for example, will prefer to offer happiness to others rather than to himself.

Thus, Stoicism tells us that we do not find happiness in glory and pleasure but in controlling our own behavior. Those who want to be happy must think about what they do and how they do it, and they must also be fair, honest, patient, humble, courageous, etc.

It is obviously good to have these values in ourselves, because they help us become a better person and get rid of our negative feelings and impulses. But sometimes actions are worth more than words. As Marcus Aurelius says:

"Don't waste any more time discussing what a good man should be. Be one."

Stoics, on the other hand, always try to act as morally as possible. They do not fear pain, death or poverty. The only thing they fear is not doing the right thing.

Seek inner peace

Stoics also seek peace and calm constantly. Specifically, the feeling of calmness within yourself.

When you do not let bad things happen and accept that some things can't be changed, you don't let them get to you. In simple terms, this means that you should remain calm, collected, and happy, no matter what happens.

As we try to achieve this calm, Epictetus gives us some advice:

"It is not a small thing that you are protecting, it is your respect, your reliability, your stability, your peace of mind, your freedom from fear and pain, in a word, your freedom. Be careful what you think."

I think it is a good thing that Epictetus places so much importance on the thoughts we have in our minds. He knows that what we do and what we feel every day is the very foundation of our freedom.

For the same experience, two people will see things very differently depending on how they perceive them. Let us look at a case in our modern world:

Peter and Paul work for the same company. Their manager wants to give them feedback on their work. So, they have a meeting with this manager. Peter is not happy with the feedback, and it makes him angry. He thinks that his superior is a fool who does not know how to do anything. Paul, on the other hand, is happy about the return. He knows that it is a comment on his work, not on him, and it will help him to improve his work and to progress.

When two people are in the same situation, one may appreciate it and the other may not. It all depends on how you look at it.

Our interpretation of what is going on in our lives gives us the impression that we are more in control of the situation. That is why working on your perception in a general way is a good thing, it allows you to see the facts in a better light.

Focus on the things you can do.

As we have just seen, Stoicism tells us that there are things we can control and things we cannot. Knowing the difference is important. So, control is particularly important.

To be happy, we must give up the things we cannot change.

For the things we can control, we must act as morally as possible and accept our mistakes, even if they are bad.

Whenever something goes wrong, it is up to us to take responsibility for it and not blame it on others.

Blaming someone else for your problems is the act of an ignorant person.

Let go of the things you cannot change.

Accept whatever comes from nature because it will happen one way or another. Despite what others think, disasters, conflicts... we still have the power to decide how we feel about these things. As for our perception, even if it does not serve us in some cases, we can always change the way we see things.

It is not the facts that hurt you that bother you, but the way you think about them. And you have the power to change that now.

One of the main reasons we get angry and unhappy, especially in our modern world, is what we want. Many people always want more. Imagine having a bigger house, a bigger car, more money. Maybe you want to be a more powerful person, or simply dream of more followers and likes on social networks.

To be happy, we must want these things. We tell ourselves that we will be happy when we have bought X or done Y. When we finally get these things, we are happy for a short while, but then we move on to another desire. In the end, we spend a lot of time in our lives not being happy or satisfied with what we are doing.

So, to be happy, we need to stop wishing for the things we do not have and be grateful for what we already have. We must learn to be grateful and appreciate the things we take for granted. Things like having a home, enough food, family, and friends.

In the morning, think about how lucky you are to be alive, breathing, and happy.

The Stoics used an exercise called premeditation to help them become more grateful. This is what we now call negative visualization. It involves imagining your life without the things you have, in order to appreciate them more.

For example, if your partner makes you breakfast every morning, imagine your life without him or her for a moment. If your partner were not there, it would be up to you to make it. Putting yourself in this mental situation can make you more grateful to that person, because you know that he or she takes time out of their day to make you happy.

Do not think about the things you do not have as if they are already there. Instead, think about how much you would seek out the things you have and how much you would want them if you did not have them.

This exercise is incredibly good. Think about what would happen if we lost everything we have. We quickly see how important they are to us and our lives, whether they are people or material possessions.

Manage your time in a way that works for you.

Many of us waste our time every day, Seneca says:

"It is not that we do not have enough time to live, but we waste a lot of it."

When we are not doing what we should be doing like working for example, we are having fun, complaining, getting angry, envying others, stressing, etc. All these moments cannot be experienced again.

We spend our time as if we had a lot of it, even though we do not.

Besides, Seneca is right when he talks about time and money:

"The way each of us gives our own life is particularly important. People are very fond of their homes and their money, but they do not give enough thought to the idea of wasting their time, which is, however, the thing we should be most careful about."

As a rule, we value money more than our time. The most important thing we have is our time, so we must protect it at all costs.

To protect our time, we must determine what is important to us and eliminate the rest. Ask yourself this question: In 10 minutes, in 10 hours, in 10 months, in 10 years, how much will it pay?

Suppose you stay on social media for 10 minutes, 10 hours, 10 months, 10 years. What will happen?

When I see other people having a "dream" life, I will probably feel bad about myself. You may not remember what you saw in a few hours, or even months or years, and it will not make any difference in your life.

Will it have influence if I watch the news for a few minutes, hours, months, or years?

My stress and anxiety might get the better of me in about 10 minutes (the media is good at that). In 10 hours, my mind may still be thinking about it, even though time has passed. In 10 months, I will have forgotten as much as I did in 10 years.

I may be able to understand something in 10 minutes. If I had worked hard for 10 hours, I might have created my first mini application. In 10 months, I will have made a complete solution. In 10 years, I'll have a business.

To put things in perspective, ask yourself the 10/10/10/10 question. This will help you determine what you should do first.

Stoicism is a practical philosophy that has been around for a long time. It helps us to live more calmly, to be at peace with ourselves and to be strong in any situation. It has many important rules, but the following five points are the most important to remember:

- To be happy, you must be fair, thoughtful, upright, and courageous. You must be tolerant and kind. You must be patient and humble at the same time.
- When we look at the world in an unusual way, we find tranquility. If we allow ourselves to be less affected by sad things, it is because we allow ourselves to be affected.
- It is important to be able to distinguish between things you can control and things you can't. Accept that some facts cannot be changed.

- Be grateful: We already have everything we need to be happy. We just need to remind ourselves of this often. For this, imagining things that are bad can help.
- Use your time wisely: We must use our time wisely because it is our most important asset. The 10/10/10/10 question can help us not to waste it. In 10 minutes, in 10 hours, in 10 months, in 10 years, what will it bring me?

Chapter 3

What is in our power?

With what we have just seen, it is legitimate to ask: what can we do? What aspects of our lives can we really change? Does it matter if we get sick or not? Do we want to have an accident one day? My loved ones are dying. How should I behave? Does it matter who we fall in love with? Can we guarantee our own success in the world? What power do we have over all these things?

How did the Stoics think about such things?

It starts with a truly clear statement of what Epictetus thinks is within our power and what is not. It is up to us to make our own decisions, to feel impulses and to want what we want. Epictetus says that most of the time we can't do anything for our bodies, our possessions, our reputation or our success in the world. He says that many people are unhappy because they misclassify things, that is, when they think they can control events when they cannot.

This division seems to involve things that are either internal or external: we can control our minds, but not the world around us. There is a significant difference between the mental and the physical. We can control our thoughts, but we cannot control things like our bodies or our possessions. There is no one right way to look at things, but both give an idea of what is going on.

Epictetus is not saying that we have control over everything in us or over our minds. Rather, he is saying that we can only control what we think about. All we can really control are our own judgments and the things that flow from them. When we think, we don't always choose the feelings or memories that come to us, and we can't always turn our emotions on or off.

There are many reasons why our judgments are so important. First, they help us decide how to act. They control our desires and impulses, as Epictetus said. We can have a specific goal and think that it is good for us, so we will give ourselves the means to achieve it. It all depends on the goal. If it's a dream job or a fancy house, it can be a much longer and harder process than other goals like eating healthy for example. It can sometimes cost us a lot of time and money. But it all starts with a simple decision to do what we think is right.

So, judgments are important, and we can't ignore them. We often make them so quickly that we don't even realize we are doing it. By judging quickly and often, we may think that the thing in question is good in itself.

But nothing outside of man can really be good in itself; what we judge is often just matter. Only a person with a good heart is truly good. The Roman emperor Marcus Aurelius, who was a great admirer of the philosopher Epictetus, often reflected on the physical nature of things that seemed good before deciding whether they were good or not. For example, a good meal is only the dead body of an animal or vegetable. Similarly, a fancy gadget or a high-end car is just a piece of metal and plastic. We value these things based on what we think of them, not on their intrinsic value.

If we want to stop judging things automatically, Epictetus explains that we can do this with a little thought and practice. Someone who can get a grip on their thoughts will have a more fulfilling life. We must decide what we want, what we need and how we act. Our happiness is therefore entirely up to us. On the surface, Epictetus seems to be saying that we don't have much control over anything, but in reality, we have control over everything that really matters to our well-being.

So, there are many other things we cannot control, like our bodies and possessions, our reputation, and how we get along in the world. In the past we have seen that the Stoics say that none of these things are good in themselves. Epictetus' view is a little different here. One of these things can make your happiness very vulnerable to outside forces. That is why you should not make your happiness depend on an event that you cannot control.

If your sense of well-being is tied solely to a romantic relationship, a specific career goal, material possessions or a certain physical appearance, then you have surrendered your happiness to the whims or needs of someone or something else. This is not a safe way to be happy.

If you think you can control these phenomena, but one day life reveals that you cannot, then you are almost certain to be frustrated and disappointed.

When Epictetus says that we should not give up or turn away from the outside world, he does not mean that we should ignore it. Just because we cannot control actions does not mean we should not pay attention to them. It is simply a matter of having the right mindset about it. Epictetus explains that you must see your life as a play. Neither you nor anyone else can choose your role. You are not allowed to make decisions, and you do not know when the event is over. It is not your job to fight all these facts that you cannot change. Your job is to play your part in the best way you can.

There are many things we do in our daily lives. It's not a good idea to stay in a bad job or keep bad relationships if deep down you don't want to. But there are other things that are more closely related to the human condition that we can't do much about, like how we feel about ourselves. The things that make us who we are will have a significant impact on how our lives unfold.

Even though we can choose how our actions turn out, we cannot always choose the consequence of our actions. People do not always get what they want or expect. Sometimes it is simply a lack of effort or work. Other times, it is because of things beyond our control.

In his writings, Antipater, a Stoic, made a comparison with archery. Even an experienced archer can sometimes miss the target because the wind can blow the arrow off course. There is nothing the archer can do about it. The same is true of medicine: no matter how good a doctor is, sometimes factors beyond his control prevent him from saving a patient. Think of all life as being like this. While we can always do our best, we can't always predict how things will turn out. If we tie our happiness to the outcome, we run the risk of being disappointed often. If our goal is simply to do our best, then nothing can stand in our way, because even our failures will become victories for us in some way.

As for events outside our lives, we can only go with the flow. It is better to let things happen and work with them than to fight against them. Marcus Aurelius says, "Nature is always changing. Nothing stays the same, and I have no power to change that." All we can do is accept what happens to us and work on the things we can change.

Epictetus is extremely strict about paying attention to what we can change. Do not worry about the circumstances that you cannot change. Instead, pay attention to your judgments, which will make you a better person, what Zeno calls "a fluid flow of life." There are times when we must pay attention. If we do not pay attention to our judgments, even for a brief time, we run the risk of reverting to bad habits.

Epictetus compares himself to a person on a boat. It is much easier for a sailor to run his boat aground than to keep it from sinking. If something bad happens to the sailor at sea, like an excessively big wave for example, he can always do everything he can to keep from sinking. But sometimes, unfortunately, a brief slackening of attention is enough to sink into the abyss.

Know what you can do.

People who follow the philosophy of Stoicism believe that there is nothing you can do about things that are out of your control. Because they are not in you, you do not know how they will turn out. The only thing you can do anything about is how you feel about those events that are out of your control.

There is nothing wrong with being angry when things do not go your way on the outside. Negative emotions, however, will not change what has just happened.

Here is a Buddhist story that fits this idea:

"The Buddha had become an enemy of Mara because of his power. So, Mara wanted to kill the Buddha. Mara's army threw stones at the Buddha, but it looked like flowers when the stones fell and hit the ground. So, Mara's soldiers shot arrows, and then flower petals were falling from the sky again. Mara could not do anything to the Buddha because he had learned to protect his happiness from outside forces. A bad thought or reaction is a rock or an arrow in your life. It is impossible to change events. But you can change how you feel about them (Monk, 2017)."

If one day you learn that you or a loved one has a serious illness, the question is not how you will feel. You can obviously be sad or upset about news like this, but it is also up to you how you react to the news. You can be sad inside but go on living your life in your own way, because your feelings won't change the fact that you are sick.

The same is true for any misfortune that may happen in our lives. As long as it is an external element that has triggered it, we cannot change the course of things. But then how do we react to these situations?

Think back to the external events that changed your life and ask yourself if you reacted in the right way to these things.

Part II

How to react to situations?

Chapter 4

Overcoming Anxiety and Criticism

In this chapter, we will focus first on anger. In general, criticism tends to make us angry, so we need to know how to deal with it in order to stay calm in any situation.

How to deal with anger

If we let anger get the best of us, it can ruin our peace of mind. As you can guess, anger cannot bring a happy feeling to your mind, so it should be avoided. So, the Stoics found ways to reduce the amount of anger we feel.

Seneca's "On Anger" is the best source of Stoic advice on how to avoid and manage anger. According to Seneca, it is not a clever idea to be angry. It is a "brief folly," which causes great harm to humans. Because of our anger, he says, we see people killed, poisoned, and sued all over the place. Cities and countries are destroyed sometimes in the anger of one man. We too can be killed by anger, or at least destroyed from within.

However, we unfortunately live in a world where there is much to be angry about. If we do not learn to control our anger, it can take over us, leaving us with a deep sense of constant unhappiness. Being angry, says Seneca, is a waste of time.

Some people think that anger has a purpose. They say that when we are angry, we are more likely to get things done in our daily lives. This is not true, says Seneca. It is true, he says, that people can get good things out of their anger. But that does not mean we should welcome it into our lives.

Notice, however, that people can also benefit from a shipwreck. But who in their right mind would then take steps to increase the chances of ending up in a wreck? It is almost impossible to extinguish or diminish the anger in us once we start using it in any circumstance. This worries Seneca, because usually the ephemeral good that anger brings will be outweighed by the harm it has caused.

"Reason will never be helped by impulses over which it has no control." Seneca

If a person sees his father killed or his mother assaulted, should he be angry? Should he or she remain stoic in the face of this situation? Not at all. He may punish the person who did wrong and protect his parents. However, he should try to stay calm while doing so. In fact, he will do a better job of "getting even" and protecting them if he does not get angry.

Seneca says that when someone does something wrong, he should be reprimanded "with gentleness and also with harshness." These corrections, however, should not be made in a bad mood. We do not punish people for what they have done because we want them to stop doing it again. We want to prevent them from doing it again. People should not use punishment as a way to show anger, but more as a way to reprimand for an action.

People who act like children when they are adults can be punished for insulting someone, for example. Seneca is quite clear on the subject: if we are dealing with someone who, even though he is an adult, behaves like a child, we might want to punish him for insulting us. The trick, again, is to remain calm in your response to this kind of person.

Let us take an example that can happen to anyone: you are walking down the street, and someone pushes you pretty hard. Instead of apologizing, the person insults you, implying that you were in the way. It can be exceedingly difficult for some people to stay calm in this kind of situation, which is understandable at first. But ask yourself: what reaction can I have that will not make things more complicated and will not let the anger build up inside me? For example, you can respond to this person calmly, making him/her understand that he/she is disrespectful, or you can simply ignore this person because you know that he/she will not change unfortunately.

This kind of person is common, those who, when they do something wrong, do not apologize.

We cannot get them to change their behavior in response to our measured and rational pleas. In this case, there is no point in getting angry and ruining our day, but it is possible to pretend to be angry.

That is what Seneca thinks. Because we can do that. We can, in rare cases, get that person to change their ways without disturbing our own peace of mind too much. Seneca does not like the idea of getting angry to get things done, but he is open to the idea of pretending to be angry to get people to do things. Be careful, however, not to actually fall into anger!

The philosopher gives a lot of specific advice on how to avoid getting angry. There are some things we should work on, he says, such as not believing the worst in others and not making assumptions about their motives. When things do not go our way, it does not mean someone has done us wrong. He says we need to remember that sometimes the person we are angry with has actually helped us. In this case, what makes us angry is that they did not help us more.

If we are overly sensitive, we are often likely to get angry too quickly. It is not just the hard things in life that we can't handle, says Seneca. If we relax too much, we can often be in a bad mood too. So, Seneca explains that we should take steps to make sure that we do not become too comfortable in our daily lives. When the Stoics say that they do not want to be comfortable, it is an understatement to say that they do not want a life that is too comfortable.

Noises from our street or a slamming door will not bother us if we are not in great comfort, making us less likely to get angry. We will not be overly sensitive to what others say or do, and we won't get angry over "trivialities" like being pushed around or having our house messed up. Let us keep our cool, says Seneca.

Keep in mind that the things that make us angry usually do not really hurt us; rather, they are annoying matters that bother us. By allowing ourselves to become angry over unimportant things, we turn what might have been a minor inconvenience into a state of agitation that cannot be calmed. As Seneca points out, "Our anger invariably outlasts the damage done to us. What fools we are, then, when we let trivial things get in the way of our peace of mind.

Some Stoics say that we should use humor to defend ourselves against insults: someone spat in the face of Cato and Socrates, and both joked. Laughter, says Seneca, is a clever way to avoid getting angry: "Laughter is the best way to deal with things that make us cry". By seeing the sad things that happen to us as funny rather than outrageous, we can make them more amusing.

An event that might have made us angry can instead make us laugh. Isn't it possible that Cato and Socrates, when they used humor in response to an insult, not only hid the insult, but also did not get angry at the person who insulted them? We can talk about repartee in these cases. Have you ever seen a person put in his place by a well-placed repartee? All without anger and full of humor? Even though repartee is something that needs to be worked on, it is an excellent weapon to fight against anger.

Marcus also gives advice on how to avoid getting angry. As we have seen, he wants us to think about how quickly the world around us is changing. Many things we think are important are not important at all, he says, at least not in the main. All over the world, people are doing the same things: getting married, having children, farming, loving, fighting, and feasting. But, he says, "of all that life, not a trace remains today. What we think is particularly important today may not be important to our grandchildren in the future. So, when we start to get angry about something, we should stop and think about its importance in the grand scheme of things. If we do this, we may be able to stop our anger in its tracks.

Suppose we try to avoid getting angry, but the actions of others make us angrier. "We are bad men living with bad men, and only one thing can calm us down: we must agree to be gentle with each other." He also gives advice on how to deal with anger that has much in common with Buddhism. When we are angry, Seneca explains, we must make sure to "transform all the signs [of anger] into their opposites." We must then force ourselves to relax our face, soften our voice, and slow down our walk. If we do this, our internal state will soon match our external state, and our anger will soon disappear. This is what we should do. Buddhists use the same technique of thought substitution.

When Buddhists have a bad thought, they force themselves to think the opposite, that is, to change that thought into a good thought. If they are angry, for example, they try to think of love. There cannot be more than one thought in a person's mind at a time. The good thought will push out the bad one, and so on.

But what happens if we cannot control our anger? Indeed, what happens if we end up giving in and yelling at the person who made us angry? We should apologize. Much of the damage that our outbursts of anger may have caused to those around us can be quickly repaired if we do this. It can also be beneficial to us personally. In addition to making us feel better, apologizing can keep us from obsessing about what made us angry. Finally, apologizing can help us become better people. It is better for us to admit our mistakes than to keep making them.

Everyone gets angry sometimes. Just as grief is an emotional response to tragic events, so is anger. But there are some people who are always in that angry state. Not only do these people get angry easily, but even when they have no reason to get angry, they do so anyway. In their free time, these people may think about events that have made them angry or that put them in that state in general. By trying to change their outlook, by trying to see these things in a more positive way, perhaps these people will become less and less angry as the days go by.

The Stoics would say that this kind of detail is sad. Life is far too short to spend it in anger. Besides, a person who is always irritated will be a pain to those around him. Why not instead, Seneca asks, "make yourself a person that everyone will love during your life and miss when you die?" To put it more simply, why not be happy when you have the power to be happy?

First, reflect on what you have done. Determine what makes you angry. Disrespect is a problem for many people, for example.

- Decide how you will handle it. According to Robertson, in moments of passion, you need to keep your humanity in mind. At the same time, be aware that you have the ability to choose how you react to situations. You can then look at the situation from a rational point of view.
- Find ways to laugh at yourself. Self-deprecation is a more modern way to do this. Avoid looking at everything the wrong way, even if the situation is bad. Look at the situation from a different angle, one that is more positive. You can think about what would happen if you got angry every time something bad or unfair happened. You

would be like a pressure cooker, always ready to explode.

- Work on distancing yourself. Seneca says that sometimes it's good to give your answer to a problem later. This is called "cognitive distancing." If a problem arises that can put you in a bad state, take a break and go for a walk. The best way to think, talk and act logically is to step back from the situation.

Overcome your anxiety

Anxiety is, like anger, a feeling that cannot be controlled. Unfortunately, we do not decide whether we will be anxious at any given time or not. However, we can reduce this everyday feeling with practice.

To combat anxiety, we must first focus on the fundamental reasons why we are anxious.

Why are we anxious? Why are we anxious? Why are we worried about the future? If we look closely at our problems, we find that all of our anxieties fall into one of two categories.

- We want what we cannot have, such as a body that never gets sick, a future that is always secure, a pleasant job that is guaranteed for life, or a reputation that is forever secure.
- We try to avoid what we cannot escape, such as old age and death.

Most of our anxieties, big or small, fall into one of two categories: anxiety about getting what we do not want and anxiety about not getting what we do want.

Anxiety is a subject that can also be dealt with by stoicism. We have talked a lot about anger, but all the examples we've seen apply equally to the life of an anxious person.

Take a situation that can put you in this state of stress: waiting for an exam. In those moments of doubt when you are wondering how you are going to get through it, ask yourself some simple questions: How can I reduce my anxiety about this event? Would studying more help me feel better? Should I do other activities to keep my mind off it?

As with a situation that makes you angry, you need to take a step back from the situation. Sometimes you may realize that the test may not be that important, or that you have done enough studying to get through it.

How do we deal with the anxiety of things we want but may not get?

The things we want are desires, big and small. We are anxious about our bodies, our appearance, our possessions, our future, and the opinions of others. We seek financial and other forms of security. We want things to go our way. We then become anxious because we know we cannot control them, because they are outside of our control. If we did control them, we would not be anxious about them, because they would be internal to us. So, it is the nature of our wants and dislikes that causes our anxiety. Desperately needing something external is a sure recipe for anxiety.

"Every time I see someone with anxiety, I ask myself, 'What does this person want?' Unless you want something that is not under your control, how can you be anxious? When you play a musical instrument alone, you don't feel any anxiety. But when you walk into a music hall, even if you have a beautiful voice and can play the instrument well, you become anxious. Not only do you want to sing well, but you want to be applauded by others, which is not under your control." - Speech of Epictetus 2.13 (Chuck Chakrapani, Stoic Choices, Chapter 2)

The best way to get rid of anxieties of this nature is to train ourselves to moderate our desire for anything we do not control. We seek external things such as money, fame and health that are not under our total control. There is nothing wrong with preferring these things to poverty, darkness or disease. However, the most important thing to realize is that external things are not under our total control. When we begin to think that we cannot be happy without them and we desperately seek them, we become anxious because we know that we may not get them. When we begin to remind ourselves, "Yes, we prefer health, wealth, reputation, etc., but we are not desperate for them," then we can be poor, have health problems, and yet be happy. As Epictetus said:

"Show me someone who is sick and yet happy; in danger and yet happy; condemned to exile and yet happy; having lost his reputation and yet happy. Show him to me, by God, I want to see a Stoic." - Speech of Epictetus 2.19 (Chuck Chakrapani Stoic Choices Ch. 19)

How do we deal with anxiety about things we do not want but could get?

The things we do not want are our dislikes. The things we dislike may include not only broccoli for some people, but also our major fears such as illness, poverty, old age, and death. If we stop disliking things, nothing we get, even if we do not want it, will make us anxious.

The best way to get rid of anxieties of this nature is to train ourselves not to dislike things we cannot control. Whenever you have an aversion to something you can't control, tell yourself, "This is nothing to me. I have the resources to deal with whatever comes my way."

Apply this to anything that causes you anxiety, such as poverty, what others think of you, illness, and even death. How can you be worried about being poor if you do not fear poverty? How can you be worried about what people think of you if you do not care what they think? How can you be worried about death if you do not fear it? How can you be anxious about poor health if you do not fear it?

As you eliminate aversions to things you cannot control, you will see this type of anxiety fade away.

How to get rid of anxiety

Now that we know why we are anxious and what to do about it, let us listen to Marcus Aurelius.

Know that you already have all the resources you need to deal with whatever comes your way. What is beyond our control is neither good nor bad. It is the way things are. You do not need things that are out of your control to be happy. There is no point in fighting reality because it always wins. There is no reason to be anxious because we will always have the internal resources to deal with whatever reality throws at us.

"Don't let the future worry you. You will face it - if you must - with reason, the same resource you use now to face life." - Marcus Aurelius, Meditations Bk. 7.8 (Chuck Chakrapani, Stoic Meditations, Book 7.8)

Know that it is easier to avoid anxieties if we stop dwelling on them. Do not be too opposed to things. When we have an aversion to things we cannot control, there is no guarantee that we can avoid them. This makes us fearful. Our fears become our anxieties. So do not dwell on your aversions.

"The cucumber is bitter? Throw it away. Are there brambles in your path? Walk around them. That is enough. Don't add, "Why do such things exist in the world?". "- Marcus Aurelius, Meditations Bk. (Chuck Chakrapani, Stoic Meditations, Ch. 8)

The cause and cure of anxiety are obvious. But to get rid of it takes practice.

Chapter 5

How to Deal with Friendship and Love

The Stoics say that friendship is one of the most beautiful things in life, because it can provide some of the most fulfilling and positive experiences that humans are capable of having.

Therefore, great thinkers advise us to choose our friendships and relationships in general carefully. In this section, I will use the terms "friendships" and "relationships" interchangeably, but these terms apply equally to a close friend, a romantic relationship, or just a friendly relationship.

Managing relationships in general

Of course, you will have acquaintances throughout your life, perhaps even "circumstantial friends", that is, people you are "friends" with simply because you are around them often. Work friends, school friends, friends who go to the same place as you. These people can be your "friends" in the philosophical sense of the word, but only after careful consideration, which you should extend to all the people you wish to consider as friends.

Seneca essentially sums up the process of choosing friends in this quote:

"If you consider as a friend a man in whom you do not have the same confidence as in yourself, you are very much mistaken and do not sufficiently understand what true friendship means... When friendship is established, you must trust; before friendship is formed, you must make a judgment... Think long and hard whether you should admit a particular person into your friendship; but when you have decided to admit him, welcome him with all your heart and soul. Speak to him as boldly as to yourself... Consider him loyal and you will make him loyal."

As you can see, then, you must deeply evaluate a person before you welcome them into your friendship, for you must be able to trust a friend as you trust yourself. Once you have made the decision to accept a person as a friend, you must welcome him or her with all your heart and soul.

This essentially means that you give them a lot of leeway because you love and forgive them as you should yourself. It is even said that by treating them this way, you can expect your relationships to grow and treat you the same way, "consider them loyal and you will make them loyal."

So, one can imagine that the lines are very wide. The line not to cross would be if the person maliciously, physically attacked you. That's when it would be reasonable to cut off the relationship. However, take a step back from the event, did your friend verbally or physically attack you for fun or was he or she under the influence of alcohol for example? Again, this boundary is up to you, but the stoics advise at least a wide margin.

Here is the answer to treating friendships as transactions or superficial.

"He who is interested only in himself, and makes friendships for that reason, is mistaken. The end will be like the beginning: he has befriended someone who could help him out of bondage; at the first click of the chain, that friend will abandon him. This is what we call "passing" friendships; the one who is chosen for his usefulness will be satisfactory only as long as he is useful... He who begins to be your friend because he brings you something, will cease to be so the day he brings you nothing. A man will be attracted by a reward offered in exchange for his friendship, if he is attracted by something in friendship other than friendship itself".
- Seneca, Letters from a Stoic

To summarize, if you treat relationships/friendships as transactions, they will always be shallow and without depth. The Stoics predict that they will end as they began, with some sort of utility provided at the beginning of the friendship, and then, once that utility is gone, the abandonment of the "relationship" because it was based only on utility.

These next three quotes explain why we should care about relationships:

"Friendship produces between us an association in all our interests. There is no good or bad fortune for the individual, we live in common. And no one can live happily if he has regard only for himself and turns everything into a matter of personal utility; one must live for one's neighbor, if one wants to live for oneself." Seneca, Letters from a Stoic.

"Nothing will ever please me, no matter how excellent or beneficial, if I have to keep the knowledge of it for myself. And if wisdom were given to me on the express condition that it should remain hidden and not be uttered, I would refuse it. No good thing is pleasant to possess, without friends to share it." - Seneca, Letters from a Stoic

"For what purpose, then, do I make a man my friend? To have someone for whom I can die, whom I can follow into exile, against whose death I can stake my own life, and pay the pledge too." - Seneca

So, Stoicism is based on the general idea that we are social beings, which is confirmed by our biology. There are very few people in the world who can truly live completely alone. It is therefore in our very nature to seek relationships.

We are also told that all the goods in the world are nothing if you do not have people to share them with. Which makes sense: what is the point of being rich, famous, beautiful, powerful or anything good, if you cannot share the benefits of those goods with others. Even in the most selfish way of boasting about your wealth, power, or fame, you need people around you, so you might as well make friends with them, even if they are of poor quality.

Finally, the ultimate goal. What is the purpose of making friends? Like all good things, we should use it to practice virtue. Without a friend, who would you have to support you, to fight in the trenches of life, to follow you through hardship, and maybe even to die? If you do not have someone to do this for, how can you practice these expressions of virtue?

Finally, Seneca tells us how creating friendships and relationships helps us and the other person in a positive way:

"Happy is the man who can make others better, not only when he is in their company, but even when he is in their thoughts" - Seneca

Being a good friend is the most likely way to influence someone's character for the better. It is the surest way to help someone become a better person. Not by lecturing someone on how they should behave, but by being a genuine and positive example. Your relationships can realize that you are a good person and be inspired by you to become one as well.

How to be a good friend?

We have just seen that it is important to surround yourself with good people, good relationships and good friends. But it is also important to be a good friend yourself.

When we think of the great Stoic figures like Marcus Aurelius, Cato and Epictetus, we tend to focus only on the individual, their point of view, their observations. But how did these brilliant thinkers treat those around them?

Historical accounts tell us that Marcus ruled the people of Rome with reason and that Cato earned the respect of his troops by sleeping with them in the trenches. Yet of all the Stoics we read today, only one has given us such a complete picture of how they spoke and acted toward their dearest friends.

Seneca's Letters of a Stoic are nothing more than a series of profound conversations he had with a close friend, each letter addressing a different topic or simply expanding on what was said in the previous letters. While this collection of correspondence allows us to know Seneca himself better, it raises as many questions as it answers. What does it mean to be a good friend? How do we maintain meaningful friendships and get rid of those that are not in our best interest to keep?

Fortunately for us, philosophers like the Stoics mentioned above have already addressed these ideas. Here are several tips from our Stoic ancestors on how to have more authentic, meaningful, and timeless friendships.

- <u>The importance of judgment in your relationships</u>

Choose the people you welcome into a relationship carefully based on their values and character.

The ability to judge situations and people is an evolutionary gift. It would not be beneficial for us to immediately trust every person we meet, as this would surely lead us to be taken advantage of.

Choosing a friend should, in many ways, be similar to the way you answer your door. When you hear a knock, you do not open the door to just anyone. For some, you leave the door closed. For others, you may open the door, but not fully. Finally, there are those you let in. Only those who have consistently proven themselves trustworthy should be allowed in. Whether it is your home or your heart, the same rules apply.

It is important to note that we become more adept at making accurate judgments over time. The Stoics called this oikeiōsis, which can be translated as "appropriation" or "familiarization."

We all begin our lives with an intact understanding of what is good and bad. We seek what is pleasant and avoid what is painful. The Stoics believed that over time we could learn to refine our sense of the good and make more accurate assessments of the natural world. Of course, this will take time and we will not always judge correctly. But the friends we judge correctly will remain in our lives forever.

- ### Do not focus on transactional relationships

Transactional relationships are doomed to fail because they are based solely on usefulness, an aspect that can easily be removed from the equation. So do not treat your relationships this way.

We all know what a fair-weather friend looks like. You share a common interest that you pursue together. You communicate here and there. It looks like friendship, but when life's difficulties come, those same friends are nowhere to be found.

We need people we can count on in times of crisis. That is why trust is such an important prerequisite for friendship. Not to mention that if we use someone for their usefulness or simply as a means to an end, we are not respecting our guiding principle of Summum Bonum. In other words, we fail to respect the values that are supposed to be embedded in everything we do.

The Stoics would undoubtedly support the pursuit of friendship because it is intrinsically good, not because it is useful. A good friend is always there when we need him. They do not back down in the face of tragedy or think they are better than the person who needs their comfort. A good friend is there, period. We need to look for this quality not only in our current group of friends, but also in ourselves.

- Aim for progress beyond your relationships

"Above all, watch this - that you never become so connected to your old acquaintances and friends that

you lower yourself to their level. If you don't, you'll be ruined. ... You must choose between being loved by these friends and remaining the same person or becoming a better person at the cost of these friends... if you try to have your cake and eat it too, you will make no progress and not keep what you had." - Epictetus, Discourse

One of the most difficult aspects of friendship is recognizing when it is time to let go. Sometimes a dear friend is still trustworthy and loyal, but his or her actions toward others and the world around him or her no longer match your morals.

In this case, we are faced with two choices. Either we maintain the friendship at the cost of our personal development, or we end it at the cost of our friendship with that person. In the first case, we choose to prevent ourselves from growing. In the second scenario, we make a difficult choice to support our values.

The Stoic response to this situation would use the idea of preferred indifference, which, in the context of friendship, would look like this: you should be neither excessively upset nor excessively joyful about the loss of a friend. Instead, you should be indifferent. For the friends we keep, we can enjoy what we hope will be a lifetime of companionship. For those we decide to let go, we do so to support our values and personal growth.

What does this mean? That we are free to embrace and cultivate whatever friendships we want, as long as they don't compromise our morality and as long as they allow us to build something constructive.

How do you build something constructive out of a relationship? By being a good friend who accepts someone wholeheartedly as you would yourself, you gain not only the joy of friendship, but also the opportunity to improve the other person by your good example. In response, this constructive goal should drive you to seek virtue, both for the benefit of the friendship and for the benefit of your friend.

- Love to share

"Nothing will ever please me, however excellent or beneficial, if I must keep the knowledge of it to myself. And if wisdom were given to me on the express condition that I should keep it hidden and not utter it, I would refuse it. No good thing is pleasant to possess, without friends to share it." - Seneca, Letters from a Stoic

If you think of some of the happiest moments in your life, chances are those memories involve people you care about. Perhaps it was the night you asked the love of your life to marry you, or the day you got your dream job and celebrated with friends and family. Whatever the occasion, one thing is certain: the best things in life are meant to be shared.

The next time you are about to do something (or anything else), try to bring a friend along. Whether it's going on vacation or watching a new show on Netflix. Listen to the joy in their voice when you invite them and fully enjoy the experience you are about to share. You will find that Seneca, as usual, was right about this too.

Remember why you have a relationship: because it is what humans naturally do, because nothing good in the world makes sense without people to share it with, and because relationships are prime opportunities to practice virtue. - Life is short

"Whenever you embrace your child, your brother, or your friend, do not superimpose upon that experience all the things you could wish for, but hold them back and stop them, just as those who ride behind triumphant generals remind them that they are mortal. In the same way, remember that your precious is not one of your possessions, but something given to you for now, not forever..." - Epictetus, Discourse

The concept of Memento Mori is well known in the Stoic community. In Latin, "memento mori" is a locution meaning "remember that you are going to die."

It is a reminder that we are not eternal, that we will die one day, and that we should by extension enjoy life.

We wear necklaces with this saying on them, we keep skull-shaped coins in our pockets, and for what purpose? To remind us that our time is limited, that what we do is important. While this mantra is designed to remind us of our own mortality, we often forget that it also applies to everyone we know.

Ask yourself if you would treat your friends the same way now, if you knew they would not be around tomorrow. It's not that we don't treat our friends well because we are petty. But we certainly lose sight of the brevity of life. We overestimate the time we have left with our loved ones. How we treat others at any given moment could be the last thing we do.

We are all good at applying the memento mori to ourselves and our own lives, but we do well to keep this in mind when interacting with our friends. If we remember to treat our companions as if they could disappear at any moment, we will be much less likely to take them for granted.

- Seek balance, not control

"Love the discipline you know, and let it sustain you. Entrust everything willingly to the gods, then make your

way through life - neither master nor slave to anyone.".
Mark Aurelius, Meditations, 4.31

Central to Stoic thought is the idea that we must understand what we can and cannot control. Perhaps the most difficult thing to accept is that we cannot control others. We have all had friends who always want to run things and order others around. They are the ones who make the plans and change them to suit themselves. In groups and competitive environments, their presence is sometimes almost unbearable.

As we seek balance, we should never play this game. We should never try to control others, nor should we allow ourselves to be controlled. Instead, we should be mindful of how we behave and accept how others are. Some of the greatest pain we feel comes from our desire to change things about someone we cannot change. What should we do? Set an example and allow our character to serve as a guide for our friends who don't always act with the same level of self-control.

The people we choose to spend our time with are a reflection of our character and our ability to judge others. As you begin to evaluate the people around you and the friends you spend time with, think about who helps you grow and who holds you back. Who can you call at three in the morning on a weekday and who will be at your door in a heartbeat? Who can you count on to lift you up when you feel like you can't get up?

Whatever your answer, friendship is one of life's greatest gifts. Having people to count on in times of crisis and to share wonderful memories with is precious in itself. Once you have welcomed someone into a relationship, welcome them wholeheartedly and fully, as you should yourself with your own strengths and flaws. Set boundaries as wide as possible. Be slow to anger and quick to forgive.

Relationships according to the ancient Greeks

Epictetus was right to emphasize the practical, but the ancient Greeks had a very sophisticated theory of love. They had many different ideas about love and friendship. It is common to say that there are four main types of love: Agape, Eros, Philo, and History.

- Agape is the kind of love you have for your spouse and children, and later Christians associated it with God's love for all. As Thomas Aquinas said, agape is wanting the best for the other person.

- The word "eros" has the primary meaning of sensual pleasure and sexual attraction. But, as Plato explains in the Symposium, Eros becomes an appreciation of a person's inner beauty, by which we show our admiration for beauty in any form.

- Our friends, family, and community are all treated equally because we treat them that way. Phila is the kind of love we feel for them that is neither selfish nor moral.

- Finally, the word "history", which is not used very often, refers to the love for your country or sports team. It means that there is a type of love that is not based on reason or thought.

The modern term "love" does not seem to encompass all these different feelings, which is a pity because we should be able to distinguish the love we have for our partner, our children, and our friends from the love we have for the country or for a God. In all cases, the Stoic question would be the same: Is this a good thing?

Sometimes we are told that we should love our country or our sports team even if they are "bad". A Stoic would say that loving something "good or bad" is different in both cases. This shows why the Stoics were right to say that certain kinds of love, such as those that are important, must be in accordance with what is right, not just our feelings about the matter.

A U.S. Navy officer, Stephen Decatur, is known for saying, "Our country! Our country! Our country! Our country! Our country!" in 1816. Whether he was right or wrong, our country will always stand by him, no matter what.

Another quote representing this would be from Carl Schurz, U.S. Secretary of the Interior, who used it in a speech before the Senate on February 29, 1872: "*My country, whether right or wrong; if right, it must be kept right; and if wrong, it must be righted.*"

The same is true of some sports team chants: "*AS Roma! With the other teams, it always comes out on top. But whatever the outcome of the game, 'AS Roma!*". There is something charming about being a fan of a sports team even if, and even more so if, they tend to lose a lot.

It is only natural that Epictetus would give the same treatment to relationships in general:

"To be a friend, one must have faith and honor. You cannot have friendship anywhere else. If someone pays attention to you, does that mean he loves you? You don't know if he will throw you away when you are no longer useful in his life."

Chapter 6

The Fatalism of Life

The Stoics thought that one way to keep our peace of mind was to consider the things that happen to us as if they were inevitable. It is a good thing that "we are carried along by the universe," said Seneca.

According to Epictetus, we must always keep in mind that we are only actors in a play written by someone else, like the Fates (the goddesses of human destiny). Our roles in this play cannot be chosen. We have to play them right, no matter what. If the Fates want us to play a beggar or a king, we must do it right. According to Epictetus, it is better to want our lives to go well than to let events unfold as we wish. In other words, we should want events to happen as they happen.

Marcus also says that we should have a good attitude toward life. If we want to live a good life, we can't do otherwise. If we want to live a good life, we cannot do anything else. Marcus says that if we do not follow the rules of fate, we may feel sorrow, anger or fear.

To avoid this, we must learn to adapt to the situation that fate has placed us in and try to love the people that fate has placed us with. It is important for us to learn to accept everything that happens to us and to convince ourselves that everything that happens to us is for the best. The good man will welcome "any experience that the crafts of fate can weave for him".

The Stoics believed that everyone had a destiny, as did most people in ancient Rome. They really believed in the importance of the three goddesses called the Fates mentioned above. They each had a role to play: Clotho creates life, Lachesis counts it, and Atropos cuts it. No matter how hard people tried, they could not change the life that the Fates had chosen for them.

They thought that life was like a horse race that had already been organized by these famous goddesses. The Fates already knew which people would win and which would fail in their lives. A jockey would probably not enter a race if he already knew the outcome of the race. Why run when someone else already knows who is going to win?

Other types of people during ancient Rome also thought that Romans did not participate in any of life's contests because the future is already fixed. What is interesting is that these people were not pessimistic about the future, even though they thought that what was to happen was to happen. The Stoics, for example, were not content to sit around and wait for the future to happen. Instead, they worked to change the outcome of future events. In the same way, the soldiers of ancient Rome bravely went to war and fought bravely in battle, even though they believed that the results of those battles were set in stone.

The Stoics advise us to take a "fatalistic" view of the things that happen to us. So, what should we think?

With this problem, we need to know the difference between fatalism about the future and fatalism about the past. When a person is fatalistic about the future, he/she always keeps in mind that his/her actions have no effect on the future. A person with this philosophy of life will therefore probably not spend much time and energy thinking about the future or trying to change it. When a person is a fatalist, they also think about the past in the same way. Since her actions cannot change the past, she will make sure to keep this in mind when deciding what to do next. Such a person is unlikely to spend much time and energy wondering how the past could have been different.

When the Stoics say that fate is inevitable, I think they are talking about a limited version of that idea. They tell us to be cynical about the past, to keep in mind that the past cannot be changed. They would not tell a mother whose child is sick to be pessimistic about the future. On the contrary, she should try to heal her child (even if the Fates have already decided whether the child will live or die). But if the child dies, they will tell the woman to be fatalistic about the past. After a child dies, even if you are a stoic, you are likely to feel sad. But thinking about the death is a waste of time and emotion because the past cannot be changed. The woman will be sad because she will think too much about the death of her child.

Many Stoics say that we should not think too much about the past. They do not mean that we shouldn't think about it at all. The past can teach us things that can help us shape the future. Because the above-mentioned mother should think about why her child died, she can better protect her other children. For example, if the child died because he or she ate poisonous berries, the mother should keep the other children away from them and teach them that they are dangerous. But after that, she should forget the past. "If only I had known she was eating those berries!" or "If I had taken her to the doctor earlier, she wouldn't have been so sick" are phrases that one unfortunately has to get out of her head.

Fatalism about the past is probably much more attractive to people today than fatalism about the future. Most of us do not believe that we are doomed to live a certain way. Rather, we believe that our efforts can change the future. At the same time, we know that the past cannot be changed, so when the Stoics tell us to be fatalistic about the past, we are unlikely to disagree with them.

The Stoics, I think, do not want us to be optimistic about the past, but want us to be optimistic about the future. Because we can't change the present, we know we can't change this moment. I can act in a way that affects what will happen in a decade, a day, a minute or even a second. For example, even if I acted in a way that changed what is happening right now, that moment would already be in the past and could not be changed.

It turns out that the Stoics told us to be fatalistic, not only about the future, but also about the past and the present. There is good reason to rethink some of the Stoic advice quoted above.

When Epictetus tells us to want things to happen "as they happen," he is giving us advice about things that are already happening, not about things that will happen. In other words, he wants us to think about the past and present in a bad way somehow.

Cynicism about the present can improve our lives in many ways. The Stoics, as I said, said that the best way to be happy is to learn to be happy with the things that are in your life right now, not to work to get your desires fulfilled.

If we allow ourselves to do this, we will spend our days wishing things were different, and that will make us unhappy. On the other hand, if we learn to desire what we already have, we will not have to work to get our desires fulfilled in order to be happy. They will already be fulfilled.

Right now, we have a big decision to make. We can spend this moment wishing things were different, or we can enjoy this moment. If we do the first thing all the time, we will be unhappy most of the time; if we do the second thing, we will enjoy our lives. To be a Stoic, we must be cynical about the present. This, I think, is why Marcus tells us that the only thing we have is the present moment, and he tells us to live in "this brief moment."

Of course, the latter advice is remarkably like the Buddhist advice that we should try to live in the moment. We should not worry about things we cannot change. We cannot change the past, and we cannot change the present, unless we are talking about this very moment. So, we are wasting our time if we worry about the past or the present.

Notice also that the advice to be fatalistic about the past and present is strangely related to the advice to practice negative visualization. Therefore, it is important to pay attention. It is a clever idea to think about how much worse our situation could be when we do negative visualization.

Our goal is to appreciate what we have. Fatalism, which the Stoics believe in, is sort of the opposite, or mirror image, of negative visualization. How our situation might get worse does not make us think about how it might get better. We act fatalistically when we think about the past and the present.

Compare our current situation to other, better situations we could have been in instead of our current situation. The Stoics believe that by doing this, we will be able to make our current situation, whatever it may be, a little more manageable.

Why work more

With this "love what you already have" ideology, one might think that Stoic thinking can make us lazy. Since Stoics are incredibly happy with what they have, no matter what the situation, why work to have new things? This is a good thing, of course. But, as a result, won't Stoics be very lazy?

In response to this, I want to remind you that the Stoics we studied were overly ambitious people by nature. As we have seen, Seneca had a continually active life as a philosopher, playwright, investor, and government advisor. Musonius Rufus and Epictetus were highly successful in running successful schools of philosophy. Marcus, on the other hand, was busy running the entire Roman Empire when he was not thinking. These people were, in a sense, gifted. It is interesting to note that even though they would have been happy with almost nothing, they still tried to get something.

Here is how the Stoics explain this "contradiction". Stoic philosophy tells us to be happy with what we have, but it also tells us to seek certain things in life. We should then try to become better people, in the sense of the word "virtuous" in the past. It is important for us to try to add stoicism to our daily life if we want to become virtuous people.

Why did Musonius and Epictetus feel the need to teach Stoicism to their students. The Stoics do not object to our taking steps to appreciate the situations in which we find ourselves. In fact, Seneca tells us to pay attention to all the advantages that come with life. We might get married and have children. We could also make friendships and enjoy them.

And what about success in the world? Will Stoics seek fame and fortune?

A Stoic probably won't. The Stoics considered these things worthless and thought it foolish to pursue such dreams, especially if it caused us to lose our peace of mind or act in a bad way. This lack of interest in worldly success, I know, will make them seem unmotivated to modern people who spend their days working hard to achieve some level of fame and fortune. That said, it is quite contradictory, but even if the Stoics didn't want to be rich, they often were.

All of the Stoics we studied were successful people in their time. Seneca and Marcus both had a lot of money and were well known. Musonius and Epictetus, who ran popular schools, were famous and probably had a lot of money. Therefore, they found themselves in a strange situation. People who did not want to be successful but still managed to be successful.

Part 3

The dangers of stoicism

Chapter 7

Becoming a Spectator of Life

Stoicism teaches us to worry about the things we control and to accept everything else as it is, being more or less indifferent. If we are upset about something external, that upset is due to our judgment and so we can get around it by changing our perspective. While these methods are great, they can also be dangerous, and I'll explain why.

Let us take an example: you are having lunch in a restaurant, you take your computer and charger out of your bag and put it next to you. A person comes up behind you and asks you for directions. As you answer him nicely, he grabs your bag and runs away.

Normally, the normal reflex would be to run after this person to try to get his stuff back, or to shout to draw other people's attention to this theft. Now let us imagine that you do neither, you remain completely stoic in the face of the situation: you remain calm and see the situation with an indifference worthy of the greatest Stoics.

The Stoic thought might be thankful that this person did not leave with your computer, but only with your bag, despite all the stuff in it. This is an exceedingly difficult reaction to have when you have just lost your wallet, important documents, or any other valuable items.

Of course, things can be worse, and so much the better if that person did not steal the computer, but isn't it dangerous to cultivate too passive an attitude? Even if it is only an object, some of them are sometimes irreplaceable, isn't it worth to react faster to this dishonest person?

Moreover, if you tell the incident to your entourage, what will be their reaction? Probably to make you understand that you were too stoic unfortunately.

Does being stoic make us weak at times? Does it make us look like strange people who can be stepped on without worry?

We should stand up straight, not be held straight, but how can we stand straight when we cannot face such simple problems? How can you have a straight spine when you let life treat you like a common doormat, people come and step on you, and in the end, you just say to yourself "people can't upset me, only my judgment can".

It is obvious that the teachings of Stoicism are still good. In most situations in our lives, it is good to remain passive in order to maintain self-control and a better view of things. But sometimes isn't it also good to respond to the bad things that happen to us?

To continue our learning lesson, we can ask ourselves: is stoicism dangerous? Does it make us passive observers of life, instead of active participants? Is it really useful to be indifferent?

Let us take an even simpler example that can happen to us every day. How should we react when someone insults us? Whether it is a friend or a person in the street, it is obviously never pleasant to be insulted.

Stoic philosophy teaches us that there is always something good in everything, that we should simply change our perception of things. But can we really accept an unjustified insult? Is there always a way to make the action good?

In the case of an unjustified insult, I think it is simply better to ignore the person, but the question could be asked in many other cases: how to react if you are pushed around or how to react if you are fired without reason?

It is particularly good to add stoicism in our lives, which is obvious, but where is the limit? I think it is up to you to choose the place that this way of thinking takes in your life. You can very well apply the rules of stoicism only in your relationships for example. It is up to you to ask yourself: where is the limit of this philosophy in my life? How far can it help me without being a danger?

Chapter 8

Poorly Defined Goals

Generally speaking, it can seem difficult to achieve our goals. In general, we tend to set goals that are too big and too ambitious. As a result, it is not uncommon to fail to achieve our life goals. Take the good resolutions we make at the beginning of the year for example. How many people forget the promise they made to themselves, only one month after promising to do everything possible to accomplish this goal?

This is not to blame, this tendency to not achieve goals is quite universal. So, let us ask ourselves: why do we fail to accomplish our goals?

Perhaps it is again a matter of perception. Let us take the eye of a Stoic to set our goals.

A Stoic's view of these goals

There are things you do not want to get, and things you cannot seem to get.

When we fail, we often blame a lack of willpower, perseverance or courage, but this is not always the case. In our minds, we think that we are not up to the task and that we were not as good as others. How can we improve to avoid thinking this?

Let us assume that we are not failing because of something within us, but rather because we are not taking the right steps. You will often be told to change your goals, but also to change the means by which you achieve them. Not only will you be more likely to achieve your goals, but you will enjoy life more in the process.

In fact, the Stoics did not think this way at all. An entire philosophy was built around thinking and acting in ways that bring out the best in people.

There are many ways to use this knowledge to achieve our goals. We need to change the way we think about goals.

What do you want to achieve? Have the best partner? Get a new job or a raise? Own a big house or a fancy car? To have fame and money?

Some 2,300 years ago, the Stoics knew that these things were what most people wanted to do. They also knew that the pursuit of these goals, sometimes quite futile, makes us feel dissatisfied. So, they thought a lot about the question of why. Why were some goals not necessarily a good thing?

Part of the reason is that these goals are bad in themselves. What the Stoics understood is that the goals we set for ourselves are often not dependent on us. Some of them depend in part on things outside of us, so we have truly little control over that goal. It is also a bad idea to set goals that are not entirely our own.

First, we implicitly rely on things outside of ourselves to work for us. Let us say we want to find the perfect partner. We hope that we are also the right partner for our right partner. If we go to a busy place where we can meet people, there is no guarantee that we will meet someone. Maybe the ideal partner didn't go out that night because he or she was just tired.

The same goes for getting rich. How many people play the lottery or other games every day hoping to win the jackpot? You cannot control the numbers that will be displayed at the end of the game, simply because it's something outside of you.

Secondly, when things outside of ourselves play a role in achieving our goals, they can cause us a lot of stress and worry. In order to get a promotion, you can't help but think about the qualifications of other candidates, how sympathetic your boss is, what others are saying about you, and what internal policies might hurt your chances. In other words, your mind will begin to swell with questions that cannot be answered satisfactorily.

Set goals that, as much as possible, you can achieve without having to worry about external elements.

What can you do to accomplish our goals?

Do the Stoics tell us anything else we should know about this? According to them, only our thoughts and actions are in our hands. So, it does not matter what happens externally, it's not in our hands. In this case, not getting a promotion, not finding a good partner, not buying your dream house and not becoming famous and rich are not necessarily good goals for a Stoic.

What if our thoughts and actions are the only things we can control? How can we apply this wisdom to goal setting?

Differentiate between process and outcome goals

Some people may want the same things we do. But Stoics may not be able to achieve their goals in the same way we usually do. Instead of focusing on what will happen, Stoics focus on what they do. They differentiate between process and outcome.

A Stoic, for example, does not worry about things that are out of his control, like office politics, gossip, or whether there are better candidates for the job. He does not think about any of that. Instead, he thinks about the kinds of things that would make him a suitable candidate for promotion, and then he begins to realize those goals.

By doing the things that make him better at what he does, repeatedly and daily, the Stoic will feel good about himself because every day he will feel good about himself.

The Stoic is better at his work because he puts all his energy and attention into it. This is also partly because he is less distracted by things that are beyond his control. Second, because he knows that mistakes and errors are beyond his control, that they are part of the process, he is less concerned about them. His goal, after all, is not to produce error-free work, but to act in a way that meets his own standards, which he can control.

As long as he meets his own standards, he does everything he can, and that's all that really matters.

If the stoic person does not get a promotion even though he has worked very hard, he knows what he is really worth and won't be afraid to look for work elsewhere, for example. The obstacle in her path is just another way for her to get around. If her boss does not see her value, someone else will.

Hard work can make us more confident and self-respecting. Overall, it makes us more competent in our field and more aware that things can change. Even if we don't get the promotion, we know that this setback doesn't take away from what we've learned by doing our job well, even if it's sometimes hard to accept.

Imagine if you could start your day worrying less about the things you cannot change, and focusing more on the things you can change, that would be a great idea to develop your sense of daily freedom.

We should focus on the things we can change, not the things we cannot. Yet, too often, we only pay attention to the things that are out there.

Stoicism is a way out. We can look at our goals in a way that fits with how the world works and how everyone is actually moving toward what they want.

To get the life you want, you must continue to pay attention to how you act each day. You will even begin to enjoy the process, because what we want to see in ourselves is change and progress. Here you will get both.

In case you do not reach your goals, try to change them instead of giving up.

You may have noticed that goals can sometimes be bad for you. Goals that are too ambitious or too many goals at once can be painful because not reaching them can hurt you.

I see this a lot in successful people. To live a meaningful life, many think you have to do a lot of things and set a lot of goals.

For example, let us take a goal of running 30 minutes a day, six days a week. If we do not have any physical activity implemented in our lives, it will seem difficult to run 6 days a week. So, let's look at this same goal with a different process.

For example, we could start by going for a walk for half an hour at least once a day. Then we could walk for 20 minutes and run for 10 minutes. By changing the process, the final goal may take longer to achieve, but it becomes much more attainable.

Another example let us say you are an entrepreneur, and you want to earn a certain amount of money per month, so you start a business. This means you have to sell a certain number of goods or services. Let us say you know how many people buy your product out of every 100 emails sent. So, you can theoretically calculate how many emails and lead interactions you need each day to reach your daily goal.

But what about larger or more general goals? Goals like, for example:

- I want to make a million dollars by the time I am X years old.
- This year I want to run a marathon.
- By the end of this year, I want to have 10,000 followers on my social network.
- I want to be happy.
- I want to get married right away.

You cannot plan or predict everything. There are some rules for setting goals.

Only when you pursue big goals that are expected to happen in the future will you feel like you have control over them. Setting goals can be dangerous. It is easy for us to believe that we can control the outcome of our lives, but that is not the case.

To achieve those big goals, it's important to differentiate the process from the outcome.

So, replace your goals with process systems. A goal is an event that will happen in the near or distant future. A system is a process that repeats itself.

Instead of focusing on where you are going, pay attention to how you will get there. Let us go back to the examples we saw earlier.

- I want to make a million dollars by the time I'm X years old.

Think about how to get rich. Is it easier to become a millionaire by working for someone or by starting your own business? Is it worthwhile to continue your education in a high-potential field? Becoming a millionaire is your goal, but instead of thinking about the money you do not have, think about how to get it.

- This year I want to run a marathon.

If you are not athletic, you know you won't be able to run a marathon in a month. Why not prepare for next year's? For example, you can start running 10 minutes a day for the first month to get into the habit of running, and then increase your running time over the months.

- By the end of this year, I want to have 10,000 followers on my social network.

You will never have that many people following you on the networks if you never publish a post. Maybe start by publishing a post a day for a few months to see if your content interests' people?

- I want to be happy.

To this broader question, you need to ask yourself what is the definition of being happy for you? If for you, being happy is simply being able to provide for yourself and being well surrounded, maybe you are already happy?

- I want to get married right away.

You suspect that you will not get married if you are single. Maybe you just need to find someone who fits you first, then consider marriage.

Is setting goals a bad thing?

As we have seen, it is quite easy to set the wrong goals. It can make us sad if we do not achieve them. So, we could legitimately ask ourselves the following question: to be happier, isn't it better not to set any goals?

To grow, we need to push ourselves out of our comfort zones. As we all know, life is meant to be lived, and you can do this if you set remarkably ambitious goals for yourself over the long term.

It does not matter if you only had 100 followers instead of 10,000, if you didn't run a marathon, if your marriage isn't working out as planned, or even if you're not happy at some point in your life.

We are our own worst enemy when it comes to being held accountable. And that can lead to tunnel vision, where we only look at our goal and get stressed when things do not go our way.

If you see that you cannot achieve your goals, do not get angry. You can always keep trying. Instead, change the way you do things. Aim for smaller goals to ultimately reach your bigger goal.

After all, goals are there for a reason, right? You want to know where you are going in life.

However, I remind you of a teaching we saw in a previous chapter: stay away from things you do not need. Having more is not always better. This is especially true when it comes to money, possessions and status. Seneca said it well:

"This person is not poor because he wants more. He is because he wants less."

Over the past few days, I've been talking with a friend, who used to be an ice skater. He has also coached Olympic athletes. We were talking about goal setting. He told me the following sentence:

"People who compete in the Olympics want to win a medal. But only a few athletes in any sport make it to the Olympics. Now, let's say you are lucky enough to get in. At the beginning of the Olympics, there are a number of people who compete for the gold medal. Only three of them will get a medal, and one person will get the gold. Not everyone can be that person. Everyone wants to achieve their goals. Even if you didn't win or reach your goals, it doesn't mean you didn't work hard."

You see, this is why I prefer to reward hard work rather than success. To me, challenging work is true success. You and I are lucky because effort is one of the few things in life that we can control.

No matter what you do or what your goals in life are, keep an eye on your efforts. In any case, do your best.

Chapter 9

Being Too Narrow Sighted

Silicon Valley Stoics describe Stoicism as the philosophy that emphasizes the Stoic teaching that wealth is an "indifferent" and that your wealth and the wealth of others is beyond your control. In fact, it is true that wealth is what the Stoics called an "indifferent," but this view comes from a superficial understanding of Stoic philosophy that does not go beyond Stoicism.

The power to do some things is in our hands, but the power to do others is not. In our power are our thoughts and feelings, as well as our motives and desires. In our power are the things we have done.

It is said that "wealth is neither good nor bad," meaning that it has no effect on a person's moral character, so he or she can prosper.

Cowardice, greed, injustice, and ignorance are not bad for anyone, no matter how rich or poor they are (courage, justice, temperance and wisdom). In other words, it is not how much money you have or how little you have that makes you morally good or bad. It's how you use it or do without it that makes the difference.

As for the Greek word eudaimonia, which can be translated as "flourishing" or "the good life," only virtue or vice can lead to it. This is what Arius Didymus says in his Epitome of Stoic Ethics.

We believe that it is increasingly common for people to misunderstand the unique Stoic concept of the term "indifferent". When virtue is set aside, the word "indifferent" takes on a whole new meaning. This is true even when Stoicism is marketed as a form of self-help. Many people in the "agency sphere" or the modern "control dichotomy" have been extremely interested in this (e.g., classics professor Margaret Graver).

This type of analysis is not interested in virtue, but only in inner calm, which comes from not being bothered by the thoughts and actions of others. Thus, "indifference" is mistakenly seen as something not worth caring about or worrying about.

Scholars of Stoicism must correct critics and enthusiasts of the philosophy when they assert that Stoics should do nothing for the good of society, or even act. This is true for critics and practitioners of Stoicism alike. Even more ironically, this type of thinking comes from Epicureanism, which was a rival philosophical school. Epicureanism claimed that the best life was one that did not cause physical or emotional pain or suffering. Epicureans believed that the best way to be free of anything that might bother them, including the problems of others, was to live virtuously (i.e., with justice, courage, temperance, and wisdom). This means that everything else, including acting virtuously, was done to achieve this.

Stoicism is not about caring or worrying about others. Otherwise, Zeno's best work would not have been his utopian version of The Republic, which describes an ideal Stoic society, not a person who is good. Zeno's Republic is not based on wealth. There is no private property, and there is no money. Taking more than we need is not a good thing to do. Because we may think we are good people, Zeno says that the ideal Stoic society is one built on the idea that we are all related to each other. Musonius Rufus said this:

"If you want to be good, you must be kind, be fair to your friends and neighbors, and care for their welfare. This is what goodness is, and this is what virtue is."

Even outside of his ideal Republic, Zeno would not promote wealth or excuse it as a "favorite indifferent." There happens to be a story in Diogenes Laertius, in which Zeno thought wealth was a "poorly chosen indifferent."

Let us look at Cleanthe, when he was still Zeno's student. The elders of Athens gave money to Cleanthe because of his good character and his philosophical knowledge, even though he was poor. He had an intellectual disability and was an immigrant. As a poor man himself, Zeno might think that he should be happy that someone else has money. Yet his response is exactly the opposite of what one might expect. He knew that Cleanthe worked hard and used cattle bones and pottery shards to write on instead of papyrus, but he also knew that Cleanthe would only use that money to hurt himself at this point. This is an important event, because Zeno thought that his protégé was talented enough to lead the Stoic school (Cleanthe led it after Zeno's death). This does not mean that Stoicism was never led by a rich person. The seventh leader, Pan Aetius, was one of the wealthiest worldlings. In the Stoic school, being rich or poor is not an obstacle to joining.

The ancient Greeks believed that their primary identity was defined by their city-state, as evidenced by the political rhetoric of their time. People like the famous ruler of Athens, Pericles, made it clear in a funeral speech that the Athenians were better than the Spartans in every way. This idea of who you are also played a role in the Peloponnesian War, which lasted just over 25 years. It was Zeno and the Stoics as a whole who saw their primary identity as being tied to the cosmopolis, that is, to the entire universe (the Divine), which by definition meant that they were tied to everyone. Hence the following:

"It is better to say "I am a citizen of the world" when asked where you are from than to say "I am from Athens

or Corinth." So why say you are an Athenian rather than just a local citizen?"

The idea of "white" as an ethnicity or "whiteness" is not only outdated, but also disrespectful of the Stoics who were cosmopolitan and moved to Athens to work. It's not hidden in a bunch of obscure Stoic bits. You can see it by looking at their names: Zeno of Cilium, Spheeris of Boorishness, Crislip of Soli, Zeno of Turkey and Diogenes of Babylon.

The use of categories, however labeled, also fails to respect the Stoic principle of bringing people into our inner circle instead of "ordering" them with boxes. Marcus Aurelius sees the danger in this, and he says:

"In the end, a man cuts himself off from the society filled with people who live near him because he is angry or dislikes them."

We use Marcus' wisdom to show how everyone can promote (or misrepresent) Stoic values to create (or endanger) a more harmonious family, workplace, and society. When a person acts for the whole of humanity, not just for his or her family, tribe, or community, he or she is also acting in his or her own best interest, which means that he or she is on the path to a fulfilling and happy life. This is reflected in our call to put people in a circle rather than a box. Those who follow the Stoic philosophy can live this way.

Chapter 10
The Real Utility of Stoicism

Stoicism was made for bad times.

It was born at a time when the world was falling apart. Stoicism was born in Athens only a few decades after the conquests of Alexander the Great and his sudden death changed the world of the Greeks. It became popular because it brought security and peace in a time of war and crisis. For this reason, the Stoic creed did not promise material security or peace in the afterlife. Instead, it promised unwavering happiness in this life.

According to Stoicism, no happiness can be secure if it is based on things that can change or be destroyed. Our bank accounts can go up or down, our careers can be good or bad, and even our friends and family can be taken from us. Whenever we choose to be brave, reasonable, or good, the world cannot get to us.

The world could take everything from us, but Stoicism says that we all have a fortress within us. The Stoic philosopher Epictetus, who was born a slave and crippled at an early age, asked, "Where is the good?" Remember, if anyone is unhappy, it is only because of himself.

Although it is natural to cry in pain, the Stoic tries to keep his or her emotions under control. He or she strives to remain happy, no matter what happens on the outside. It is a hard way to live, but the reward is freedom from passion - freedom from the emotions that often seem to control us when we should be in charge of them. A true Stoic is not cold. Even though he knows that fear, greed, and sorrow only come to mind when we choose to think about them. Stoicism says it is because they only come into our minds if we let them in.

As if it were meant for a world that is at its wit's end, like the chaotic world of ancient Greece or the financial crisis of the modern world. It does not matter. Epictetus would say that as long as we try to find happiness in things that can be lost, our worlds remain on edge.

Stoicism is made for the world.

The world that gave birth to Stoicism was a small and isolated place. Most people clung to the old divisions of nationality, religion, and status, and they did not want to change them. If we find it strange to embrace our differences, we can thank Stoicism for that. It was perhaps the first Western philosophy to say that everyone should be brother and sister. We are all at home in our country and in the city of gods and men. Epictetus said that every person is a citizen of both places. The most famous Stoic in history, Marcus Aurelius, told himself every day to love the world as much as he loved his hometown.

If the key to happiness really lies in our own will, then even the greatest social divides begin to look small when we think this way. "Remember that the person you call your slave comes from the same stock, that the same skies smile upon him, and that, on equal footing with you, he breathes, lives, and dies." It was on this subject that the Roman stoic Seneca asked his compatriots to reflect.

Under the Roman Empire, a wide range of ethnicities and religions came together for the first time. Stoicism was the perfect philosophy for this, as it embraced cosmopolitanism, which means "world city." Stoicism made sense in a more global world, and it still does today.

After going to prison for over seven years, Stockdale said that Stoicism saved his life. He had studied Stoic thought for years before he went to war. When he was in captivity, he turned to these teachings to help him cope. Stockdale's Stoic practice helped him deal with the sad reality of his situation without becoming depressed or hopeless.

Some people in the military used Stoicism as a source of strength. Stockdale was not alone. Nancy Sherman, who taught philosophy at the Naval

Academy. She said stoicism is a big part of the military mindset, especially when it comes to things like endurance, self-control, and inner strength.

A philosophy for being a leader.

Stoicism says that before we try to control things, we must first control ourselves. Our efforts to have an effect on the world are subject to chance, disappointment and failure. But self-control is the only one that can work 100% of the time. Throughout history, leaders have found that a stoic attitude helps them gain respect even when they fail and protects them from arrogance when they succeed. This explains why Marcus Aurelius was a good emperor.

Stoicism is a viable choice for anyone who has to deal with uncertainty, which we all do. Leaders must deal with a lot of different things, so it's not surprising that many of them find a Stoic attitude important to their mental health. In an interview with Michael Lewis, Barack Obama showed that he has a very stoic personality:

"I try to make fewer decisions. I don't want to make decisions about what I eat or what I wear, because I have too many other things to think about."

You cannot pay attention to all the little things throughout the day. Regardless of what you think of Obama's policies, this is typical of stoicism: trying to figure out what is important and what is not in all aspects of life.

It is true that stoicism doesn't always work. As a child, Bill Clinton read Marcus Aurelius' Meditations. He is not the first person one would imagine to be a Stoic, but he was a great fan of the philosophy.

In his youth and until his death, Cato the Younger remained faithful to this philosophy. He had however fit of anger, stubborn pride, and occasional alcoholism. On the other hand, he was the most courageous when he faced Julius Caesar's army and ensured its defeat without batting an eyelid. He lived up to the ideals of the Stoics.

The more we use Stoic qualities in good times, the more likely we are to find them in ourselves when we need them most.

Staying humble in the face of difficulties

As we have just seen in many aspects, adding this philosophy to your life can do a lot for you.

Understanding stoicism, for example, helps you understand the nuance between annoyance and persistence. If you are spending more time than you should on a personal project, perhaps a little persistence, without getting angry, could go a long way in helping you accomplish that task.

No matter what you are aiming for in life, whether you have big goals, small ones, or none at all, you will face many difficulties. Becoming a more stoic person will allow you to overcome many of the obstacles that will stand in your way, while remaining humble.

A person who is able to work steadily, remaining humble and calm in the face of difficulties, gives people confidence. It is by remaining calm in all situations that you will be able to master them better later on.

Conclusion

I hope you enjoyed reading this book as much as I enjoyed writing it. The serenity of stoicism can really help you maximize your happiness and overcome your problems.

Now that you have been introduced to Stoicism, I urge you to try to implement it into your life.

Take some time and think about what is in your power. What can you change about your life? Can you afford to? What new things can you add to your life to make it better?

Think about your relationships, your surroundings, your life. Does this make you happy? Free yourself from the anxiety that may have taken its place in your daily life. Also think about how you can become a better person. Everyone wants to have the best people around them, but maybe you need to start with yourself, being a good person to others.

Life is short, so look for balance in your life. Work on it more to make it fit your image. Finally become the person you want to be.

Think back to all your goals that you have not yet accomplished. Reinvent them so that they become much more attainable. It is better to work on your goal a little bit every day, rather than getting sick of it by trying to force things too quickly.

Stoicism is an excellent philosophy of life to introduce into your life. Even if you have to be careful with the few dangers it can bring, a little bit of this ideology in your daily life will only improve it, or at least stimulate your life a little more.

More generally, let us all become good people. Whether you follow these teachings or not, the conclusion of this book would be you have much more control over your life than you think. Finally, I would conclude with this sentence from Epictetus:

"How long will you wait before you demand the best for yourself?"

Printed in Great Britain
by Amazon

24183248R00069